U.S. ENVIRONMENTAL PROTECTION AGENCY
OFFICE OF INSPECTOR GENERAL

I0428792

## Evaluation Report

# EPA Needs an Agency-Wide Plan to Provide Tribal Solid Waste Management Capacity Assistance

Report No. 11-P-0171

March 21, 2011

**Report Contributors:**

Ganesa Curley
Jeffrey Harris
Rebecca Matichuk
Thane Thompson

## Abbreviations

| | |
|---|---|
| AIEO | American Indian Environmental Office |
| EPA | U.S. Environmental Protection Agency |
| FTE | Full-time equivalent |
| FY | Fiscal year |
| GAP | Indian General Assistance Program |
| GPRA | Government Performance and Results Act |
| IHS | Indian Health Service |
| OECA | Office of Enforcement and Compliance Assurance |
| OIG | Office of Inspector General |
| OSWER | Office of Solid Waste and Emergency Response |
| RCRA | Resource Conservation and Recovery Act of 1976 |
| w/STARS | Web Sanitation Tracking and Reporting System |

**Cover photos:** *from left*: A typical dump site usually found in remote forested areas within reservation boundaries; an open dump site on tribal lands in California; a reservation open dump site that has caught fire. (EPA photos)

U.S. Environmental Protection Agency
Office of Inspector General

11-P-0171
March 21, 2011

# At a Glance

*Catalyst for Improving the Environment*

## Why We Did This Review

We conducted this evaluation to determine whether the U.S. Environmental Protection Agency's (EPA's) tribal solid waste management activities are helping tribes develop the capacity they need to eliminate open dumps.

## Background

Illegal dumping of solid waste poses significant health and environmental risks to the members of 564 federally recognized Indian tribes throughout the country. Currently, there are nearly 4,000 reported open dumps located on tribal lands. EPA has been working for over 25 years to help tribes develop the capacity to manage solid waste and enforce against illegal dumping. This work is facilitated through the Office of Solid Waste and Emergency Response, the Office of Enforcement and Compliance Assurance, and the American Indian Environmental Office.

**For further information, contact our Office of Congressional, Public Affairs and Management at (202) 566-2391.**

**The full report is at:**
www.epa.gov/oig/reports/2011/
20110321-11-P-0171.pdf

## *EPA Needs an Agency-Wide Plan to Provide Tribal Solid Waste Management Capacity Assistance*

### What We Found

EPA cannot determine whether its efforts are assisting tribal governments in developing the capacity to manage solid waste or reduce the risks of open dumps in Indian country. EPA's performance measures do not assess whether the Agency's efforts are effective in building solid waste management capacity in Indian country. EPA also lacks internal data controls to track the status of open dumps.

EPA does not have an Agency-wide plan that defines the roles and responsibilities of the EPA program offices and regions. EPA also lacks internal controls that hold these offices accountable for providing consistent solid waste management assistance to tribes. The lack of a single, Agency-wide plan results in poor coordination and limited oversight, and may lead to an ineffective use of resources. As a result, EPA cannot (1) ensure that consistent solid waste management assistance is provided, (2) accurately determine the risks of open dumps, or (3) determine whether efforts are effective nationwide.

### What We Recommend

We recommend that the EPA Deputy Administrator develop an Agency-wide plan to implement consistent and effective tribal solid waste management capacity assistance. We recommend that this single plan outlines the roles and responsibilities of EPA program offices and regions, and identifies the Agency resources required for these activities. The plan should also implement output and outcome measures that track how consistently and effectively EPA activities are provided for tribes. Further, this plan should include (1) internal controls to ensure consistent data collection, (2) a process to ensure coordination between EPA program offices and regions, and (3) a timeline specifying when the activities and outcomes outlined in the plan are expected to be accomplished.

The Agency did not agree with our conclusion or most of the recommendations in the report. The Agency did not agree to develop a national plan to manage and implement tribal solid waste management capacity assistance. EPA did agree to identify resources required for providing solid waste assistance and to improve program office coordination. However, EPA rejected recommendations aimed at improving data collection, outcome measures, and internal management controls. These recommendations will remain unresolved until such time as the Office of Inspector General and EPA can reach agreement on required actions.

UNITED STATES ENVIRONMENTAL PROTECTION AGENCY
WASHINGTON, D.C. 20460

March 21, 2011

## MEMORANDUM

**SUBJECT:**    EPA Needs an Agency-Wide Plan to Provide Tribal Solid Waste
Management Capacity Assistance
Report No. 11-P-0171

**FROM:**    Arthur A. Elkins, Jr.
Inspector General

**TO:**    Bob Perciasepe
Deputy Administrator

This is our report on the subject evaluation conducted by the Office of Inspector General (OIG) of the U.S. Environmental Protection Agency (EPA). This report contains findings that describe the problems the OIG has identified and corrective actions the OIG recommends. This report represents the opinion of the OIG and does not necessarily represent the final EPA position. Final determinations on matters in this report will be made by EPA managers in accordance with established audit resolution procedures.

The estimated direct labor and travel costs for this report are $364,610.

**Action Required**

In accordance with EPA Manual 2750, you are required to provide a written response to this report within 90 calendar days. You are also required to submit a corrective action plan for agreed-upon actions, including milestone dates, within 120 calendar days. The OIG may report recommendations left unresolved after 180 days to Congress in our Semiannual Report, as authorized by Office of Management and Budget Circular A-50. Your response will be posted on the OIG's public website, along with our memorandum commenting on your response. Your response should be provided as an Adobe PDF file that complies with the accessibility requirements of section 508 of the Rehabilitation Act of 1973, as amended. The final response should not contain data that you do not want to be released to the public; if your response contains such data, you should identify the data for redaction or removal. We have no objections to the further release of this report to the public. We will post this report to our website at http://www.epa.gov/oig.

If you or your staff have any questions, please contact Wade Najjum at (202) 566-0832 or najjum.wade@epa.gov, or Jeffrey Harris at (202) 560-0831 or harris.jeffrey@epa.gov.

# *Table of Contents*

## Chapters

## Appendices

# Chapter 1
## Introduction

## Purpose

The overall objective of this review was to determine whether the U.S. Environmental Protection Agency's (EPA's) tribal solid waste management activities are helping tribes develop the management and enforcement capacity they need to eliminate open dumps.

## Background

Open dumping is the depositing of solid waste anywhere (on land or in water) other than an approved solid waste facility. Open dumping may pose significant health and environmental risks to the members of 564 federally recognized Indian tribes[1] throughout the country. Public health and environmental concerns from open dumping of solid waste may include the degradation of tribal resources, an increased incidence of disease, food and drinking water contamination, and air pollution. The number of reported open dumps located throughout Indian country has grown from approximately 600 in 1994 to nearly 4,000 in 2010.[2]

Tribal governments, as well as the federal government, are responsible for regulating the environment and protecting the health, welfare, and resources of tribal members on reservations and other tribal lands. However, tribal governments frequently lack the infrastructure, management capacity, or economic means to sustain private or public waste-removal services. Open dumping can come from people who reside outside the tribal community and dispose of their waste on tribal lands to avoid regulated dumping fees. Additionally, the "checkerboard" land status of many reservations and tribal lands can impact whether a tribe can manage waste or enforce against illegal dumping. For example, EPA states that tribes often find it difficult to regulate the waste management activities on lands owned by nonmembers within the tribal community. This inability to manage waste or enforce against illegal dumping could result in open dumps.

---

[1] For the purposes of this report only, the terms "tribal government(s)" and "tribe(s)" refer to federally recognized tribal governments within the contiguous United States. Tribal governments are recognized by the U.S. Department of the Interior (73 Federal Register 18553 (April 4, 2008)).

[2] This report refers to "Indian country" as defined in 18 U.S.C. §1151, meaning: (a) all land within the limits of any Indian reservation under the jurisdiction of the U.S. government, notwithstanding the issuance of any patent, and including rights-of-way running through the reservation; (b) all dependent Indian communities within the borders of the United States, whether within the original or subsequently acquired territory thereof, and whether within or without the limits of a state; and (c) all Indian allotments, the Indian titles to which have not been extinguished, including rights-of-way running through the same. Various federal statutes may use or define other terms (e.g., reservations) that will control the applicability of a particular statute in Indian country.

## Solid Waste Regulatory Authority in Indian Country

The Resource Conservation and Recovery Act of 1976 (RCRA), amending the Solid Waste Act, established programs governing the disposal of solid and hazardous waste. Under RCRA Subtitle D (Solid Waste), EPA established national standards for solid waste disposal and the operation of solid waste landfills. Facilities not meeting federal standards are considered open dumps and should be closed or upgraded using regulatory authorities. However, EPA is not authorized under RCRA to implement solid waste programs for states or tribes.

States are responsible for permitting and monitoring municipal and nonhazardous waste landfills. States have also developed EPA-reviewed programs that apply to all operators of sites within the state. However, EPA explained that state programs generally do not apply in Indian country. According to EPA, RCRA defines tribes as "municipalities"; therefore, tribal governments are ineligible to be treated as states. As a result, EPA has no authority to require, operate, or enforce solid waste programs for tribes; EPA can only assist tribes in developing solid waste programs under their own tribal sovereignty.

RCRA does provide EPA with two enforcement authorities to address open dumps. Section 7003 authorizes EPA to abate specific conditions found at a site that may pose an imminent and substantial endangerment. Section 4005 (c)(2) allows EPA to enforce solid waste regulations at facilities with household hazardous waste or small quantity generator waste in any state that has not adopted an adequate program.

## EPA's Tribal Solid Waste Management Activities

As discussed above, EPA does not have the authority to implement or enforce solid waste programs in Indian country. As a result, the Agency can only assist tribal governments in developing integrated solid waste management programs. EPA can also pursue direct enforcement to address specific incidences of open dumping. Within EPA, the Office of Solid Waste and Emergency Response (OSWER), the Office of Enforcement and Compliance Assurance (OECA), and the American Indian Environmental Office (AIEO) assist EPA regions in implementing these programmatic activities provided for tribal clients.

### Office of Solid Waste and Emergency Response

OSWER provides technical assistance to help tribes develop solid waste programs. This technical assistance includes training, outreach materials, and educational resources. OSWER also supports regional EPA staff in addressing the development of tribal solid waste programs. EPA informed us that 7.5 full-time equivalents (FTEs) have been allocated nationally to the regions since fiscal year (FY) 1999. The 7.5 FTEs have been divided among the regions to close open dumps, help tribes develop integrated waste management plans, provide regulatory and program assistance, and make site-specific flexibility requests for proposed tribal lands. Further, OSWER facilitates cross-program and federal agency partnership efforts to integrate activities, provide grant funding, and leverage resources to address solid waste management in Indian country.

## Office of Enforcement and Compliance Assurance

OECA provides compliance and technical assistance to help tribal governments meet federal environmental regulations. Assistance focuses on waste enforcement capacity, including solid waste code development and enforcement training. OECA also pursues enforcement for specific dumping incidences when a responsible party is identified. From FY 2008 through FY 2010, OECA issued the National Indian Country Compliance Assurance and Enforcement Priority: Illegal Dumping focus area (OECA Indian Priority). Under this priority, regions provide compliance assistance to improve the enforcement capacity of tribes and pursue enforcement options to reduce risks from open dumps.

## American Indian Environmental Office

AIEO oversees the Indian General Assistance Program (GAP). GAP provides tribes with grant funding for planning, developing, and establishing environmental protection programs. GAP is the primary and most significant source of EPA funding to support solid waste activities in Indian country. In particular, GAP can be used to implement solid and hazardous waste programs on tribal lands. In FY 2009, GAP received about $62 million to assist the 564 federally recognized tribes. On average, each tribe receives about $110,000 per year to build management capacity across multimedia environmental programs. With respect to GAP grants, in most cases tribes give priority to capacity building for drinking water and wastewater activities, rather than solid waste management.

## *EPA's Responsibilities Under the Indian Lands Open Dump Cleanup Act of 1994*

The Indian Lands Open Dump Cleanup Act of 1994 (Open Dump Act) directed the Indian Health Service (IHS) to (1) identify the location of open dumps on Indian and Alaska Native lands, (2) assess the relative health and environmental hazards posed by such dumps, and (3) provide financial and technical assistance to Indian tribal governments and Alaska Native entities to close such dumps in compliance with applicable federal or Indian tribal government standards and regulations. The act also directed IHS to work cooperatively with EPA in the study and inventory of open dumps on Indian and Alaska Native lands. This work includes listing the geographic location of all open dumps, evaluating the contents of each dump, and assessing the relative severity of the threat to public health and the environment posed by each dump. In 1994, Congress found at least 600 open dumps on Indian and Alaska Native lands.

## Prior Audit Reports

Prior EPA Office of Inspector General (OIG) reports have evaluated Agency waste management and capacity development efforts in Indian country. In Report No. 2004-P-00003, *Immediate Action Needed to Address Weaknesses in EPA Efforts to Identify Hazardous Waste Sites in Indian Country*, issued January 30, 2004, we found that the Agency's efforts to inventory hazardous waste sites on tribal lands needed immediate action. Specifically, the Agency's efforts had been substantially delayed due to project mismanagement issues. Inventory-related information needed to manage its Superfund activities in Indian country had not been defined. The Agency also had not developed a detailed plan for validating, managing, storing, or updating the baseline inventory. OSWER concurred with our recommendations to provide oversight, define specific program needs, and develop a detailed plan for the maintenance of its inventory.

In Report No. 2007-P-00022, *Promoting Tribal Success in EPA Programs*, issued May 3, 2007, we noted that innovative practices maximize the effectiveness of tribal environmental programs. We recommended that the EPA Assistant Administrator for Water work with tribes to promote innovative practices. The recommended practices included collaboration and partnerships, accessible education and outreach materials, and identification of economic resources and funding alternatives. The Agency agreed that the recommendations we outlined would lead to an improved level of tribal successes.

In Report No. 08-P-0083, *Framework for Developing Tribal Capacity Needed in the Indian General Assistance Program*, issued February 19, 2008, we found that many tribes had not developed long-term plans describing how they would use GAP funding to build environmental program capacity. Further, we found that EPA had not tracked the progress of the plans that were in place. EPA also did not consider tribes' capacity needs and prior progress when allocating funding. We recommended that the EPA Assistant Administrator for Water develop and implement an overall framework for achieving capacity, require regions to work with tribes to develop environmental plans that reflect intermediate and long-term goals, and revise the manner in which GAP funding was distributed to tribes. EPA concurred with these recommendations.

## Noteworthy Achievements

EPA facilitates the Tribal Solid Waste Interagency Workgroup[3] to coordinate federal agency assistance. This assistance helps tribes to comply with solid waste

---

[3] The workgroup also includes representatives from the U.S. Department of the Interior, Bureau of Indian Affairs; the U.S. Department of Health and Human Services, Indian Health Service; the U.S. Department of Agriculture, Rural Development; the U.S. Department of Housing and Urban Development; and the U.S. Department of Defense.

regulations, establish integrated waste management programs, and close open dumps. Federal assistance is provided through the Tribal Solid Waste Management Assistance Project in the form of grants, cooperative agreements, loans, technical assistance, and use of equipment. Since FY 1999, the workgroup has funded over 187 projects valued at approximately $23 million.

EPA Regions 5, 8, and 9 help tribes by leveraging technical assistance and funding across EPA programs and other federal agencies. EPA Regions 5, 8, and 9 have also developed innovative resources and tools to help tribes develop and implement solid waste programs. For example, a Region 5 resource guide identifies federal funding and technical assistance available to support construction of waste collection and disposal infrastructure on tribal lands.[4] The Region 8 *Sustainability Evaluation Tool* helps tribes assess the long-term capacity of their solid waste programs. The Region 9 *Tribal Solid Waste Costing Tool* workbook helps tribes determine the economic feasibility and costs/user fees associated with tribally operated collection services, transfer stations, and landfills.

## Scope and Methodology

We conducted this performance evaluation in accordance with generally accepted government auditing standards. Those standards require that we plan and perform the evaluation to obtain sufficient, appropriate evidence to provide a reasonable basis for our findings and conclusions based on our objectives. We believe that the evidence obtained provides a reasonable basis for our findings and conclusions based upon our objectives. We conducted this evaluation from November 2009 to September 2010.

The scope of this evaluation is limited to the authorities and responsibilities delegated to EPA through RCRA, the Open Dump Act, and GAP.

To address our objectives, we reviewed relevant regulations, policies, strategies, and guidance. These documents outline the federal government's trust responsibility to tribal governments, solid waste enforcement and funding authorities, strategic measures, interagency agreements, and solid waste management and enforcement activities in Indian country. We also reviewed relevant open dump data, compliance assurance and enforcement data, and budget information.

During this evaluation, we interviewed tribal solid waste program and enforcement managers and staff in OSWER, OECA, AIEO, and EPA Regions 5, 8, and 9. We conducted roundtable discussions with environmental department staff from tribes located within these regions. We also interviewed the associate director of the Division of Sanitation Facilities Construction from IHS.

---

[4] EPA does not have the authority to fund construction or capital expenditures for tribes.

We selected three EPA regions for this evaluation because it was not feasible to meet with all regions and federally recognized tribes. It was also not feasible to include Alaska Native Villages because of their unique environmental and solid waste management challenges, as well as their remote location. We selected EPA Regions 5, 8, and 9 because they represent a cross-section of urban, suburban, and rural dumping issues. The tribes in these regions are in varying stages of solid waste program development. More than 200 federally recognized tribes reside within EPA Regions 5 (35 tribes), 8 (27 tribes), and 9 (147 tribes). These three regions account for over 80 percent of all tribal lands within Indian country.

# Chapter 2
## EPA Cannot Determine Whether Solid Waste Management Activities Are Effective

EPA cannot determine whether its activities are consistently or effectively assisting tribal governments to develop solid waste management capacity. EPA does not have sufficient performance measures that track whether tribes receive assistance that focuses on all the elements of a successful tribal solid waste program, or measures that assess whether the Agency's efforts are improving tribes' waste management capacity. EPA also cannot accurately determine the universe of open dumps or their associated risks. Finally, EPA does not have an Agency-wide plan that defines the roles and responsibilities of EPA program offices and EPA regions, and EPA has no internal controls that hold these offices accountable for providing consistent solid waste management assistance to tribes. As a result, EPA is unable to determine whether its efforts are reducing the environmental and human health risks posed by open dumps in Indian country.

## EPA Measures Are Not Sufficient to Determine Whether Tribes Are Receiving Consistent and Effective Capacity Assistance

EPA has identified five elements[5] of a successful tribal integrated solid waste management program:

1. Solid waste management plans
2. Solid waste codes, ordinances, or regulations
3. Enforcement mechanisms
4. Viable solid waste disposal options
5. Community outreach and education

According to EPA, the degree to which these elements are implemented typically indicates a tribe's capacity to manage solid waste. However, EPA does not have measures to support and track tribes' development and use of each program element. OSWER only monitors the solid waste management plan element, and OECA's measures cannot determine whether compliance assistance is helping tribes develop solid waste codes and enforcement mechanisms. Without measures linked to each element, EPA cannot determine whether its efforts are improving solid waste management capacity in Indian country.

---

[5] EPA's *Tribal Decision-Maker's Guide to Solid Waste Management* discusses the five capacity elements in more detail.

### OSWER Strategic Targets Do Not Adequately Measure Tribes' Solid Waste Management Capacity

Under Goal 3 of EPA's FY 2006–2011 Strategic Plan, OSWER is expected to achieve the following tribal solid waste targets by FY 2011 over the FY 2006 baseline:

1. Increase by 118 the number of tribes covered by an integrated waste management plan.
2. Close, clean up, or upgrade 138 open dumps in Indian country and on other tribal lands.

OSWER's current strategic targets only include output measures that track the level of activity that will be provided over a period of time, and do not connect to outcome measures that track the intended results of carrying out its program or activities.[6] For instance, OSWER's first target counts the number of solid waste management plans adopted by tribes, regardless of whether the plans have been implemented. Even though having a plan is the first capacity element of a successful solid waste management program, this target neither determines whether the Agency's efforts are consistent and effective in developing successful plans nor tracks whether the plans are effective tools for managing solid waste after they are implemented by tribes.

OSWER's second target focuses on closing or upgrading dumps. However, this target does not determine whether tribes have developed the management capacity to prevent new open dumps from occurring or to prevent former dumps from reappearing on tribal lands. This target is also not aligned with the Agency's resources and authority. EPA's primary source of funding for solid waste activities in Indian country is GAP. However, GAP provides tribes with grant funding for planning, developing, and implementing solid and hazardous waste programs on tribal lands. Further, the Open Dump Act directed IHS to be the lead federal agency to provide financial and technical assistance to close these sites, while directing EPA to assist IHS in the study and inventory of open dump sites on tribal lands. Although closing and upgrading open dumps reduces the environmental and health risks, OSWER's primary responsibility is to provide technical assistance to help tribes develop solid waste programs.

One of the regions we interviewed suggested additional measures to OSWER to assess tribal capacity, but these measures have yet to be adopted. Another region we interviewed told us that OSWER's goal of increasing the number of tribes covered by a plan would be difficult because the measure is outside the control of

---

[6] The 1993 Government Performance and Results Act (GPRA) specifically defines performance measures as indicators, statistics, or metrics used to gauge program performance. GPRA also describes outcome measures as the intended result of carrying out a program or activity and output measures as the level of activity that will be provided over a period of time, including a description of the characteristics (e.g., timeliness) established as standards for the activity.

the regional staff. While regional staff can encourage tribes to develop integrated waste management plans, the staff stated that the plans are not required and must be voluntarily developed by each tribe. According to OSWER, the current strategic targets were created because the results can be quantified. However, without measures that track all the elements of a waste management program and the results of the Agency's efforts, OSWER cannot determine whether EPA's efforts are effectively developing solid waste management capacity on tribal lands.

### OECA Measures Cannot Determine Tribal Enforcement Capacity or Environmental Outcomes

The OECA FY 2008–2010 Indian Priority directed regions to use compliance assistance to improve the solid waste enforcement capacity of tribes and enforcement to reduce open dump risks. To meet these goals, OECA established two performance measures:

1. Provide solid and/or hazardous waste compliance/technical assistance to 20 percent of tribes each year in FYs 2008, 2009, and 2010.

2. By the end of each fiscal year, EPA will conduct 10 enforcement investigations to determine the appropriateness of enforcement actions to address specific incidents of illegal open dumping in Indian country.

Regions provide compliance and technical assistance to emphasize tribes' development of waste management plans with solid waste codes and enforcement programs. In FYs 2008 and 2009, 239 and 234 tribes, respectively, received solid or hazardous waste compliance or technical assistance on one or more occasions. However, OECA's assistance measure only tracks the number of tribes "reached."[7] This output measure does not track how many of these tribes actually achieved the goal of developing codes or enforcement programs. This measure also does not identify the compliance activities, tools, or technical assistance regions should provide to help tribes achieve this goal. As a result, OECA cannot determine which activities are successful and use its resources to support the most effective compliance activities.

Waste investigations help EPA work with tribes to identify open dumps, responsible parties, and enforcement options. From FY 2008 through FY 2009, EPA regions conducted 20 waste investigations.[8] Like the OSWER measures,

---

[7] The OECA *Guide for Addressing Environmental Problems: Using an Integrated Strategic Approach* (March 2007) states that both outcome and output measures should be established for any priority area. The guide defines outputs as product or service delivery targets that can include the number of tools developed, clients reached, and activities conducted. Outcome measures assess changes in understanding, behavior, or environmental condition resulting from outputs. Outcome measures serve as the primary indicator of progress toward achieving the goal.

[8] "Investigation" was defined as region outreach to tribes to identify dumping incidents in which there may be responsible parties. Based on the type of waste and media potentially affected, regions were to consider enforcement options to accomplish waste removal.

OECA's output measure only counts the number of waste investigations conducted. OECA does not measure any resulting improvements in the ability of tribes to enforce against illegal dumping, compliance, or environmental conditions. Our review of the outcomes of EPA waste investigations conducted during FYs 2008–2009 found that:

- Six investigations did not provide sufficient information for EPA to pursue a waste investigation for illegal dumping or open dump sites for which there may be a responsible party.
- Two investigations conducted could not identify or locate responsible parties for the purposes of analyzing enforcement options.
- Six investigations resulted in site compliance or cleanup without EPA enforcement. As a result of these investigations, four tribal governments were able to initiate or work directly with responsible federal agencies and other parties for waste removal or disposal.
- Four investigations analyzed EPA enforcement options and resulted in the cleanup of one dump site by a tribal government.
- Two investigations yielded both a responsible party and sufficient evidence for EPA to take direct enforcement actions under environmental statutes. Of these, EPA enforcement action resulted in the elimination of 12,678 cubic yards of annual solid waste discharge.

In addition to output measures, EPA needs outcome measures to determine whether its assistance is developing the necessary solid waste management capacity in Indian country to prevent and reduce the risks from open dumps. Currently, EPA is relying on output measures as proxies for outcomes to determine whether its activities are effective. However, OSWER and OECA output measures cannot determine whether EPA's tribal solid waste management efforts are effective. Further, OSWER's measures do not capture or track how OECA compliance and enforcement activities directly contribute to waste management plans and open dump closures. Unless EPA improves its measures, the Agency cannot ensure that resources are used to provide consistent and effective assistance for tribes.

## EPA Cannot Accurately Track the Status of Open Dumps

The Open Dump Act directed EPA to work cooperatively with IHS to study and inventory open dump sites on Indian lands. EPA has partnered with IHS to maintain the web Sanitation Tracking and Reporting System (w/STARS)[9] for collecting and archiving open dump data.[10] EPA uses this database to track progress toward meeting its strategic target of closing, cleaning up, or upgrading open dump sites in Indian country. As of April 2010, the w/STARS database

---

[9] The Operation and Maintenance Data System module of w/STARS archives the open dump data.

[10] Open dump data include (1) location of dump sites, (2) status (i.e., closed, cleaned up, remediated, open, and active), and (3) health hazard information.

reported 3,884 sites. The distribution of the open dump universe across the EPA regions is shown in figure 1.

**Figure 1: Distribution of w/STARS open dump sites across EPA regions**

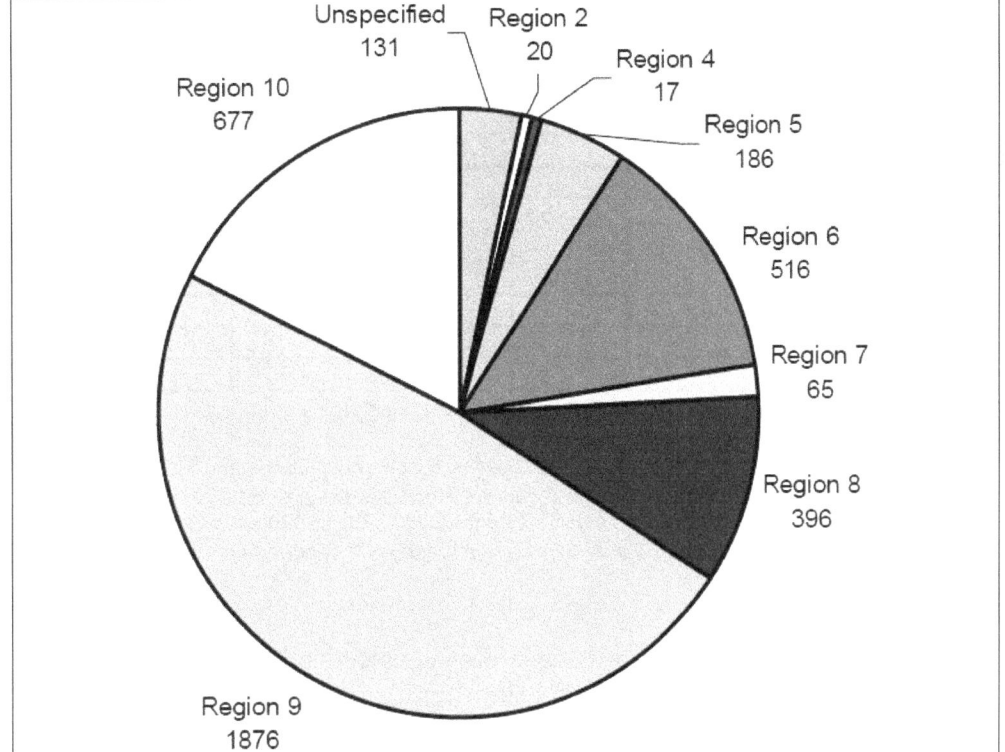

Source: IHS w/STARS database, as of April 2010. The "Unspecified" category represents missing information. Regions 1 and 3 do not have any reported open dumps.

The w/STARS database also has the capability to track health hazard information for each of the reported open dump sites in Indian country. Health hazard information includes the characteristics of each dump site, such as rainfall, site drainage, frequency of burning, controlled access, public concern, vertical distance to drinking water aquifer, and horizontal distance to surface water bodies or homes. This information is used to calculate a site's health threat score and designate a health threat level (i.e., low, moderate, or high) in w/STARS. As of April 2010, 207 active open dump sites, or 9 percent of the active open dump universe, had "high" health threat levels. The distribution of health threat levels for active sites across the EPA regions is shown in table 1 below.

Table 1: Health threat levels at active sites from the w/STARS database

| EPA region | High | Moderate | Low | Total sites with health threat | Unknown[a] |
|---|---|---|---|---|---|
| Unspecified[b] | 19 | 40 | 3 | 62 | 27 |
| 1 | 0 | 0 | 0 | 0 | 0 |
| 2 | 3 | 12 | 2 | 17 | 0 |
| 3[c] | n/a | n/a | n/a | n/a | n/a |
| 4 | 0 | 0 | 1 | 1 | 0 |
| 5 | 0 | 0 | 162 | 162 | 5 |
| 6 | 58 | 85 | 144 | 287 | 41 |
| 7 | 4 | 8 | 13 | 25 | 4 |
| 8 | 40 | 75 | 59 | 174 | 127 |
| 9 | 17 | 33 | 1,224 | 1,274 | 48 |
| 10 | 66 | 95 | 162 | 323 | 1 |
| Total | 207 | 348 | 1,770 | 2,325 | 253 |

Source: IHS w/STARS database, as of April 2010.

[a] The "Unknown" category includes open dump sites without health threat scores.
[b] The "Unspecified" category includes open dump sites that have not been associated to an EPA region within the w/STARS database because of missing information.
[c] Region 3 does not have any federally recognized tribes.

EPA is using the incomplete w/STARS database to track progress toward meeting its open dump target. As shown in figure 1, about 3 percent of the reported sites in w/STARS had not been associated to an EPA region because of missing information. Further, table 1 shows that about 10 percent of the active open dump sites (253 sites) do not have a designated health threat level. Regions 5, 8, and 9 stated they have completed their initial open dump inventories. However, these regions stated that not all the health hazard information is complete or accurate. The regional and tribal environmental department staff we interviewed also stated that they lack the resources to conduct thorough field assessments or open dump activities tied to this target.

EPA also lacks sufficient controls[11] to ensure the quality, objectivity, utility, and integrity of open dump data information. For instance, EPA lacks Agency-specific guidance outlining how regions should gather, manage, and utilize these data. The regions we interviewed use IHS guidance to collect and input data into the w/STARS database. However, EPA has not developed its own guidance outlining when the IHS data collection forms should be filled out and updated, who should fill out the forms, which data fields are necessary to collect for EPA's tracking

---

[11] The Office of Management and Budget defines internal controls as an integral component of an organization's management that provides reasonable assurance that the following three objectives are achieved: (1) effectiveness and efficiency of operations, (2) reliability of financial reporting, and (3) compliance with applicable laws and regulations. Internal controls also include the plan of organization; methods and procedures adopted by management to meet its goals; and processes for planning, organizing, directing, controlling, and reporting on agency operations (see Office of Management and Budget Circular No. A-123).

purposes, and how the Agency should prioritize its open dump efforts given its limited resources. Further, the staff we interviewed stated that the Agency lacks a clear national definition of what constitutes an "open dump," which has resulted in the regions having different methods for collecting and reporting open dump information.

EPA does not have a complete database and sufficient internal data controls to accurately track the status of open dumps. As a result, the Agency cannot determine whether it is collecting open dump data consistently and effectively across the regions, whether cleanup efforts are effective, or whether it is using open dump data to prioritize work and leverage its limited resources. Without accurate and complete open dump information, EPA will be unable to determine the relative environmental and human health risks.

## EPA Does Not Have an Agency-Wide Plan to Provide Solid Waste Management Capacity Assistance

EPA's role is to help tribal governments develop solid waste management programs and pursue enforcement for specific incidences of illegal dumping. To do this, the Agency provides technical assistance, grant funding, and solid waste management assistance. These activities are provided by EPA regions at the direction of three separate program offices. We found that EPA does not have a national-level process to ensure that program offices and regions are accountable for providing consistent and effective solid waste management assistance for tribes.

OSWER's guidance and strategies[12] outline how regions should reach EPA's strategic plan targets. However, the guidance and strategies do not provide sufficient detail to help regions track and prioritize solid waste work. Moreover, OSWER's approach does not provide requirements for the way in which EPA should coordinate efforts across program offices or with other federal agencies. Further, OSWER does not have an effective and standardized process to collect and disseminate outreach documents, evaluation tools, and national pilot programs. As a result, EPA has no assurance that it can avoid duplicating efforts or wasting its limited resources.

OECA's Indian Priority directs regions to use compliance assistance to improve the solid waste enforcement capacity of tribes and enforcement to reduce risks from open dumps. However, OECA's performance measures do not provide regions with guidance on how and when to use specific compliance and enforcement assistance tools and resources to meet these goals. These measures

---

[12] OSWER has the OSWER Tribal Strategy, issued in 2008; and the Office of Solid Waste and Regional Tribal Integrated Waste Management Strategy, issued in September 2007. In 2009, the Office of Solid Waste became the Office of Resource Conservation and Recovery, which is located within OSWER.

only hold regions responsible for the number of activities conducted. OECA does not have any outcome measures to hold regions accountable for achieving results. Varying levels of staff technical expertise or resources to analyze and pursue enforcement options may further impact the consistency of waste investigations and results. As a result, OECA cannot ensure that tribes have the opportunity to access a consistent and effective range of assistance across regions.

While most of EPA's tribal solid waste program activities are provided by OSWER, AIEO, through GAP, manages the primary source of EPA funding for tribal capacity building. However, AIEO does not have sufficient guidance[13] and systems in place to ensure that GAP funding is consistently and effectively used among the regions for building solid waste capacity. For instance, AIEO lacks sufficient guidance for how GAP staff should coordinate with OSWER program staff to ensure that resources are used consistently and effectively to achieve Agency targets. Further, the staff we interviewed stated that AIEO follows the Annual Commitment System dates, but AIEO does not have the responsibility of setting or projecting targets for solid waste activities. Without sufficient oversight and internal controls, EPA cannot determine whether the GAP funding used for solid waste activities is effective in developing solid waste management capacity in Indian country.

Without an Agency-wide plan, EPA's efforts will continue to result in poor coordination and limited oversight, and may lead to an inefficient use of resources. Lack of internal management controls further limits the Agency's ability to hold specific program offices accountable for achieving and tracking outcomes. Until EPA develops an Agency-wide plan to provide solid waste management activities, the Agency cannot ensure its efforts are consistent or effective.

## Conclusions

Incomplete measures prevent EPA from determining whether its efforts are developing the necessary solid waste management capacity to prevent open dumps in Indian country. EPA's lack of internal data controls prevents the Agency from effectively tracking and prioritizing open dumps with the highest environmental and health risks. Finally, EPA does not have a single Agency-wide plan that collectively defines the implementation roles and oversight responsibilities of the EPA program offices and regions. As a result, EPA cannot determine whether it is providing consistent or effective solid waste management assistance activities in Indian country to reduce the public health and environmental risks posed by open dumps.

---

[13] AIEO has issued the following GAP guidance to headquarters and regional solid waste and tribal staff and the National Indian Work Group: (1) *Implementation of Solid and Hazardous Waste Activities under the Indian Environmental General Assistance Program*, issued June 2001; (2) *National Program Recommendations for Use of GAP Funds for Implementation Activities*, issued June 2001; and (3) *Indian General Assistance Program 2006 Grant Administration*, issued February 2006.

# Recommendations

We recommend that the Deputy Administrator:

1. Develop and implement an Agency-wide plan for providing consistent and effective tribal solid waste management capacity assistance that is within the scope of EPA's authority and responsibility.

2. Require that the Agency-specific plan include:

   a. Descriptions of the roles and responsibilities for the EPA program offices and EPA regions conducting solid waste management capacity assistance activities in Indian country.
   b. Identification of the Agency resources required for providing solid waste management assistance activities.
   c. Performance measures, including both output and outcome measures, to track whether its assistance is consistent and effective in developing solid waste management capacity and reducing risks from open dumps in Indian country.
   d. Internal controls to ensure consistent data collection and consistent provision of waste management capacity assistance to tribal clients nationwide.
   e. A process to ensure coordination between EPA program offices and regions.
   f. A timeline specifying when the activities and outcomes outlined in the plan are expected to be accomplished.

# Agency Comments and OIG Evaluation

The Agency disagreed with our first recommendation. EPA stated that the OIG had assessed the Agency's programs in isolation from the significant efforts conducted by the IHS. EPA said IHS has the primary authority and significant responsibilities to assess and close open dumps. We agree that IHS is considered the lead federal agency under the Open Dump Act. However, the Agency misinterpreted our conclusion and recommendation. We have reworded the recommendation, requesting that EPA develop an Agency-wide plan that falls within the scope of EPA's authority and responsibility.

The Agency also rejected all but two of the actions listed in our second recommendation. EPA agreed to identify resources required for providing solid waste assistance (subpart b), and agreed to improve program office coordination as necessary (subpart e). However, EPA rejected recommendations aimed at improving data collection, outcome measures, and internal management controls. These recommendations will remain unresolved until the OIG and EPA can reach agreement. The Agency's detailed response with the OIG's evaluation is provided at Appendix A.

# Status of Recommendations and Potential Monetary Benefits

| | | RECOMMENDATIONS | | | | POTENTIAL MONETARY BENEFITS (in $000s) | |
| Rec. No. | Page No. | Subject | Status[1] | Action Official | Planned Completion Date | Claimed Amount | Agreed To Amount |
|---|---|---|---|---|---|---|---|
| 1 | 15 | Develop and implement an Agency-wide plan for providing consistent and effective tribal solid waste management capacity assistance that is within the scope of EPA's authority and responsibility. | U | Deputy Administrator | | | |
| 2 | 15 | Require that the Agency-specific plan include: | U | Deputy Administrator | | | |
| | | a. Descriptions of the roles and responsibilities for the EPA program offices and EPA regions conducting solid waste management capacity assistance activities in Indian country. | | | | | |
| | | b. Identification of the Agency resources required for providing solid waste management assistance activities. | | | | | |
| | | c. Performance measures, including both output and outcome measures, to track whether its assistance is consistent and effective in developing solid waste management capacity and reducing risks from open dumps in Indian country. | | | | | |
| | | d. Internal controls to ensure consistent data collection and consistent provision of waste management capacity assistance to tribal clients nationwide. | | | | | |
| | | e. A process to ensure coordination between EPA program offices and regions. | | | | | |
| | | f. A timeline specifying when the activities and outcomes outlined in the plan are expected to be accomplished. | | | | | |

[1] O = recommendation is open with agreed-to corrective actions pending
C = recommendation is closed with all agreed-to actions completed
U = recommendation is undecided with resolution efforts in progress

# *Agency Comments and OIG Assessment*

December 6, 2010

MEMORANDUM

SUBJECT:     Response to the Office of Inspector General Draft Evaluation Report: "EPA
                      Needs an Agency-Wide Plan to Provide Consistent Tribal Solid Waste
                      Management Capacity Assistance," Project No. OPE-10-0002

FROM:          Robert Perciasepe
                      Deputy Administrator

TO:               Jeffrey K. Harris
                      Director for Program Evaluation, Cross Media Issues
                      Office of Program Evaluation
                      Office of Inspector General

Thank you for the opportunity to comment on the draft evaluation report of September
24, 2010, entitled "EPA Needs an Agency-Wide Plan to Provide Consistent Tribal Solid Waste
Management Capacity Assistance," Project No. OPE-10-0002 ("Draft Evaluation"). On behalf of
the Environmental Protection Agency (EPA or Agency), I want to thank the Office of Inspector
General (OIG) for its suggestions for improving the Agency's efforts regarding tribal solid waste
management programs, including compliance assurance and enforcement activities.

We appreciate the attention that the OIG has placed on evaluating the Agency's current
solid waste management and compliance assurance and enforcement programs in Indian country.
The Draft Evaluation correctly notes the numerous waste management challenges that tribes
face, including the lack of waste management infrastructure and the economic resources to
sustain adequate waste collection and removal programs. Thus, many tribes have experienced
significant open dumping issues.

It is important to take note of the fact that EPA has in place a strategy for improving
waste management in Indian country (*Office of Solid Waste (OSW) and Regional Tribal
Integrated Waste Management Strategy,* September 10, 2007.) To supplement that strategy, we
agree that the Agency's efforts would benefit from additional, specific, planning activities that
are national in scope to ensure programmatic consistency and effectiveness. However, we have
an overarching concern that the Draft Evaluation has examined EPA's efforts and responsibilities
regarding tribal solid waste management programs in isolation from the significant efforts of
other federal agencies. In particular, the Indian Health Service (IHS) has authority and
significant responsibilities to assess and close open dumps, and to assist in funding the
construction and operation of solid waste facilities. Although EPA has provided valuable
technical assistance to tribes through grants for integrated waste management planning, hosting
national and regional meetings to provide training and hired circuit riders who provide on-site

advice, the Agency does not have similar broad authorities for assisting construction and operation of solid waste facilities in its support role to IHS, and has limited funding and enforcement authorities for closing open dumps. This consequently constrains the Agency's efforts in this area. Thus, we believe it would be helpful for the OIG to more fully describe and consider the complexities that exist as these programs are implemented. The Agency also commits to identify and clarify EPA authorities for implementing solid waste management programs in Indian country. We have responded to the specific recommendations below. We have also included an attachment intended to correct and clarify certain elements of the Draft Evaluation.

**OIG Response:** The objective and scope of our review was to determine the effectiveness of EPA activities to develop tribal solid waste management capacity and eliminate open dumps. We evaluated EPA's responsibilities under RCRA and GAP, as well as the specific efforts and responsibilities that support IHS under the Open Dump Act. Our report recommends actions that will improve EPA's contributions to the significant efforts of other federal agencies.

### OIG Recommendation 1: "Designate a program office to develop a national plan for providing consistent and effective tribal solid waste management and enforcement services."

Response:  Because we have an important role with respect to solid waste issues in Indian country, EPA commits to: 1) continue to implement its strategy (as noted earlier) for improving waste management in Indian country and 2) initiate the national planning activities discussed in this memorandum that are within its purview, taking into consideration the resources that are available to build tribal solid waste program capacity and enforce federal environmental laws in Indian country. Given the complex nature of the legal and jurisdictional issues arising among federal, tribal, and state entities, the focus of the Agency's national planning activities will be on the evaluation of established measures, internal controls, internal Agency coordination, and clarification of funding authority under the Indian General Assistance Program (GAP). These activities are distinct from the actions of federally recognized Indian tribes (tribes), tribal members, non-tribal members and other federal agencies, particularly IHS. The Office of Solid Waste and Emergency Response (OSWER) and the Office of International and Tribal Affairs (OITA) will be the lead program offices for coordinating these national planning activities among OSWER, OITA, the Office of Enforcement and Compliance Assurance (OECA), other EPA offices, the Regions, and other federal agencies.

While we recognize the benefits of developing a national plan that would address solid waste management and enforcement activities in Indian country, we do not concur with the Draft Evaluation's recommendation that EPA develop a national plan that would include the actions listed in the other recommendations. Although EPA recognizes that it has an important role in supporting the resolution of solid waste issues, EPA is not the lead Federal Agency for the issue of unaddressed solid waste problems in Indian country and cannot accept the responsibility for completion of a comprehensive national plan to address those issues. Specifically, IHS, pursuant to the Indian Lands Open Dump Cleanup Act of 1994 (Open Dump Act), has specific authority to provide financial and technical assistance to Indian tribes and Alaska Native entities to close open dumps ; currently the IHS database shows that there are approximately 3,400 open dumps nationwide. In addition, the Open Dump Act requires IHS to develop an inventory of all open dump sites on Indian lands and Alaska Native lands, and report to Congress annually on the level of funding needed to effectively close or bring into compliance all such open dumps. (See 25 U.S.C. § 3903(4)(b).) Furthermore, under the Indian Sanitation Facilities Act, 42 U.S.C. § 2004(a), IHS is authorized to construct solid waste sanitation facilities, establish utility organizations, and fund the operation and maintenance of solid waste facilities. EPA's role regarding these activities is more limited and is primarily to assist IHS in their efforts in the assessment of open dumps. Thus, if a national plan were to be produced regarding the provision of tribal solid waste management services, we believe that it should be through an interagency effort led by IHS with EPA as a participant and contributor. We will engage further with IHS, as well as other federal agencies, and will convene an interagency senior level meeting to discuss how EPA and the other federal agencies can work in concert to address solid waste issues on Indian lands.

**OIG Response:** The Agency interpreted our recommendation to develop a "national plan" as being outside the scope of EPA's authority and responsibility. We believe the Agency interpreted this recommendation as meaning that EPA should take the primary responsibility to create a national plan that all federal agencies would abide by when addressing solid waste issues in Indian country. This recommendation was intended to be specific to EPA and within the scope of EPA's authority. We are recommending that EPA develop and implement a unified agency plan that would apply to all EPA program offices and EPA regions responsible for solid waste management capacity and enforcement in Indian country.

We believe EPA is responsible for addressing this recommendation because EPA has developed Agency strategies and priorities for waste management and compliance assistance. EPA also reports achievements under GPRA goals for the variety of activities provided to tribes that lead to dump closure. RCRA Subtitle D also provides EPA with two enforcement authorities to address open dumps, and the Agency can assist tribes in developing solid waste programs under their own tribal sovereignty. Further, EPA provides tribes with funding to develop and implement solid and hazardous waste programs under GAP.

**OIG Recommendation 2a: "Implement a national plan that includes resources required to provide solid waste management and enforcement services and designate the source of those resources."**

Response: The Agency will identify the resources available within EPA, and the sources of these resources to build tribal solid waste program capacity and enforce federal environmental laws within RCRA's statutory framework. This effort will be conducted in parallel to the ongoing efforts of OITA to revise the GAP guidance and distribution process to place more emphasis on tribes' prior progress, environmental capacity needs, and long-term goals. (See "Framework for Developing Tribal Capacity Needed in the Indian General Assistance Program Report," No. 08-P-0083, February 19, 2008.) The Agency recognizes that tribes receiving GAP funds are given the ability to spend these funds on capacity building that can include solid and hazardous waste activities specific to their individual environmental priorities. Further, as the authorizing statute allowed, tribes may use GAP funds for purposes or programs that "include the development and implementation of solid and hazardous waste programs for Indian lands." Under Report No. 08-P-0083, the Agency is revising the GAP Administration Guidance and intends to include additional guidance specifying the solid waste management activities that can be funded.

**OIG Recommendation 2b: "Implement a national plan that includes output and outcome measures linked to intended results."**

Response: The Agency agrees that the tribal program performance measures should be linked to the intended results and believes that the existing measures are consistent with this goal. The Agency, however, will evaluate and analyze the current measures to see if any additional or different measures are needed in this regard.

The Agency, however, disagrees with certain elements in the Draft Evaluation's finding leading up to this recommendation, because we believe the current Indian country measures are linked to the intended results and do show results. For example, OECA's Indian Country Priority compliance/technical assistance measure is a capacity development outcome measure. Activities underlying this measure emphasize two things: (1) compliance and technical assistance for developing tribal integrated waste management plans with enforceable codes aimed at deterring illegal dumping and open burning of wastes; and (2) helping tribes understand how to comply with RCRA. Likewise, assistance to tribes from OSWER and OITA for the development of integrated waste management plans also is a capacity development function. An increase in the number of tribes with integrated waste management plans, as reported through the Annual Commitments System, is evidence that EPA's assistance is achieving its intended results. Through the end of FY 2010, 117 tribes have established integrated waste management plans which meet the Agency's definition under the GPRA goal. Moreover, the current EPA guidance regarding this measure generally addresses the tribal program areas which the Draft Evaluation highlights as aspects of a successful tribal program.

Also, we would note that EPA's enforcement actions are not intended to build tribal capacity, but to compel clean-up or closure as necessary at a specific facility. By definition, hazards are reduced when open dumps are upgraded or closed, whether or not the hazard or exposure reduction is quantified. The cost to calculate reduced hazard and exposure for each site cleaned up, closed or upgraded would divert limited resources from enforcement actions that actually address open dumps. EPA believes that the number of cleaned up, closed or upgraded open dumps is a useful and appropriate proxy for quantification of reduced hazard (under the current GPRA goal, 565 open dumps have been reported as cleaned up, closed or upgraded since the beginning of FY 2007). The Agency developed its current measures recognizing the limitations of its authority. The further analysis of measures also will recognize these limitations, as well as the need to ensure the measures and goals are quantifiable, measurable, and within EPA's control.

**OIG Response:** To determine the achievement of Agency goals, EPA needs outcome measures to track whether EPA's assistance is effectively developing the necessary solid waste management capacity in Indian country to prevent and reduce the risks from open dumps. Based on the Agency's response, EPA is currently relying on output measures as proxies for outcome measures to determine whether its efforts are effective. We found little connection between the outputs provided and the outcomes claimed by the Agency. For example, OSWER is counting the number of waste management plans adopted by tribes, regardless of how effectively the tribes are implementing those plans. The Agency states that this OSWER measure is also sufficient to capture how compliance assistance contributes to tribes' development of enforceable codes, which is just one element of a waste management plan. However, OECA output measures only count the number of tribes "reached" through compliance assistance and the number of enforcement investigations (defined as outreach to tribes) conducted. Without additional outcome measures, it is unclear how the Agency can determine that compliance assistance leads to enforceable codes, or determine what portion of the achievements claimed under OSWER's plan measure are actually attributable to OECA's efforts.

OSWER also counts the number of cleaned up, closed, or upgraded open dumps without determining whether tribes have developed the management capacity to prevent new open dumps from occurring or prevent former dumps from reappearing. The Agency believes that OSWER's open dump closure measure is a sufficient proxy for quantification of reduced hazard as a result of enforcement. However, OSWER's measure does not capture how OECA investigations and enforcement actions directly contribute to or are linked to open dump closures.

The Open Dump Act directed EPA to work cooperatively with IHS in maintaining the open dump database (i.e., w/STARS), which should be instrumental in quantifying the open dump problem in Indian country. We do not believe, however, that OSWER's open dump closure measure ensures that these efforts are building solid waste management capacity in Indian country or that these efforts are aligned with the Agency's resources. As a result, we continue to believe that EPA needs to reevaluate and develop appropriate measures that are in alignment with the Agency's authority, activities, and resources.

**OIG Recommendation 2c: "Implement a national plan that includes internal controls to ensure consistent data collection and services to tribal clients nationwide.**

Response: The Agency agrees with the Draft Evaluation's statement that internal controls are important, and commits to determining whether additional internal controls are necessary. For example, EPA will determine whether any additional information is needed beyond the existing IHS protocols and the detailed survey form used to assess open dumps and enter data regarding open dumps into the IHS data system. We believe that the concern underlying this recommendation is that the assessment of open dumps is ongoing and incomplete. For example, many open dumps that are listed in the database have not received a full assessment or had an assessment prior to the development of the current database and the associated protocols. In both cases, the data pertaining to those sites will remain incomplete pending a new assessment. IHS, in cooperation with EPA, is responsible for conducting these assessments. However, the Agency also will provide clarification on what constitutes an open dump for the purpose of EPA's entries into the IHS data system and the strategic measure.

EPA disagrees, however, with the specific references to inconsistent data collection pertaining to open dumps. The inventory of open dumps maintained by IHS includes specific guidance for analyzing and inputting data based on multiple risk factors. EPA, through a cooperative agreement with IHS, assists with data input and does so according to the IHS guidance. The Agency will continue its efforts to work with IHS and individual tribes to conduct assessments of open dumps in Indian country, and to collect the associated data.

An example of where the Agency's current internal controls are in place is within OECA. OECA sets national policies for, and establishes measures related to providing compliance assistance, conducting compliance monitoring (e.g., investigations), and pursuing appropriate enforcement in Indian country. Under the solid waste focus area of EPA's National Compliance Assurance and Enforcement Priority, OECA developed compliance assistance and investigation measures as benchmarks for undertaking specific activities to improve compliance with RCRA, build tribal solid waste capacity, and identify whether an enforcement action is the appropriate approach to addressing specific incidents of illegal dumping. At midyear and end of year from fiscal year (FY) 2008 - 2010, OECA received a report from each Region containing results for each measure.

EPA also does not agree that either the Draft Evaluation's background information or its recommendations support the conclusion that the lack of "national internal controls" has led to "poor conditions" in Indian country, "limited oversight" by Agency officials, or the "ineffective use of resources." In fact, the Draft Evaluation does not make a finding that the Agency's use of resources has been ineffective in improving a tribe's waste management capacity or reducing the risks posed by open dumps.

**OIG Response:**  The Agency lacks internal controls that include (1) an Agency-wide plan that defines missions and responsibilities, goals, and objectives; (2) processes for planning, organizing, directing, and controlling program operations; and (3) systems for measuring, reporting, and monitoring program performance.

EPA is using the incomplete w/STARS database to track the Agency's open dump closure measure. While we recognize that the database is not static, our primary concern underlying this recommendation is that the Agency lacks plans, processes, systems, or other related internal controls to manage these data. EPA needs specific procedures outlining when the IHS data collection forms should be filled out and updated, who should fill out the forms, which data fields are necessary to collect for EPA's tracking purposes, and how the Agency should prioritize its open dump efforts given its limited resources. EPA does not have these controls in place and cannot determine whether it is using its resources to collect the open dump data consistently and effectively nationwide. Without this information, EPA cannot ensure its efforts are developing solid waste management capacity and reducing risks in Indian country.

In addition, OECA's national policies lack the internal controls to ensure regional accountability for providing access to a consistent range of solid waste codes and enforcement assistance. For instance, the varying technical expertise of EPA staff and resources across the EPA regions impacts the availability of assistance provided to tribes. Further, OECA's measures cannot be used as sufficient internal controls. Specifically, OECA's assistance measures only hold the Agency responsible for counting the number of tribes "reached" and the number of waste investigations conducted by the Agency. However, these measures do not provide the Agency with a plan, processes, or systems for how the Agency should provide consistent and effective compliance and enforcement assistance to achieve the intended results.

Finally, we did not report that "the lack of 'national internal controls' has led to '*poor conditions*' *(emphasis added)* in Indian country. Our "At a Glance" section states, "The lack of a single plan results in **poor coordination (emphasis added)** and limited oversight, and may lead to an ineffective use of resources." With regard to oversight and efficiency, we refer to the body of this response above to support EPA's need for more effective measures and internal controls (i.e., oversight methods). Further, if EPA does not have effective measures and internal controls in place, the Agency cannot assure that it is using its resources as effectively as possible.

**OIG Recommendation 2d: "Implement a national plan that includes a process to ensure coordination between EPA program offices and regions."**

Response: The Agency believes that the numerous existing coordination activities, including regular meetings, conference calls and personal contacts, are effective. However, we also believe that improvements always can be made, and as a component of these planning activities, the Agency will examine its existing internal coordination efforts and make any necessary changes and improvements.

**OIG Recommendation 2e: "Implement a national plan that includes a specific timeline within which outcomes are expected to be accomplished.**

Response: The Agency proposes the following timeline:

| | |
|---|---|
| Consistent with the Agency's response outlined above, OSWER and OITA will be the lead program offices for coordinating the national planning activities to: <br> 1. Identify and clarify EPA authorities for implementing solid waste management programs in Indian country. <br><br> 2. Identify the internal EPA resources and their respective sources available to build tribal solid waste program capacity and enforce federal environmental laws within RCRA's statutory framework; <br><br> 3. Review the ongoing GAP Administration Guidance revision effort to insure correlation with the national planning activity efforts described in this response; <br><br> 4. Analyze EPA's current performance measures and evaluate the need for additional or different performance measures to ensure linkage to the desired results; <br><br> 5. Re-examine the existing internal EPA controls to ensure consistent data collection and provide additional information to the Regions regarding the assessment of open dumps which have not received an assessment under the recent IHS protocols; <br><br> 6. Clarify what constitutes an open dump for the purpose of EPA's entries into the IHS data system and the strategic measure; and <br><br> 7. Examine EPA's existing internal coordination efforts and make any necessary changes and improvements. | FY 2011 – 2012 |
| The Agency will implement the results of these national planning activities as necessary. | FY 2012 – 2013 |

**OIG Response:** EPA's corrective action plan will need to commit to an Agency-specific national-level plan with the elements and internal controls outlined in the recommendations, as well as a timeline for its design and implementation.

# *Distribution*

Office of the Administrator
Assistant Administrator for Enforcement and Compliance Assurance
Assistant Administrator for International and Tribal Affairs
Assistant Administrator for Solid Waste and Emergency Response
Regional Administrator, EPA Region 5
Regional Administrator, EPA Region 8
Regional Administrator, EPA Region 9
Agency Followup Official (the CFO)
Agency Followup Coordinator
General Counsel
Associate Administrator for Congressional and Intergovernmental Relations
Associate Administrator for External Affairs and Environmental Education
Director, American Indian Environmental Office
Audit Followup Coordinator, Office of the Administrator